"You need someone else to be a rock star, to be cool. You can totally be yourself."

MILEY CYRUS to the *National Post*

For Jess, the sister I never had.

Photographs © 2009: Anthony Cutajar: 16 foreground, 22, 39 top left, 53, 103 center left, 104; **AP Images:** 72 (Chris Polk), 98 (Matt Sayles); **Corbis Images:** 1, 90 right, 91 bottom (Rune Hellestad), 95 (Scott Lituchy/Star Ledger), 6 right, 8, 9, 11, 48, 88 top (Andrew Mills/Star Ledger), 10, 46, 47, 102 top right, 102 center right (Tim Mosenfelder), 79 (John Zich/zrImages); **Courtesy of Daisy Rock Girl Guitars:** 31, 102 center; **Everett Collection, Inc./PAX:** 102 bottom left; **Getty Images:** 100 (Evan Agostini), 35 background (Vera Anderson), 32 (Brad Barket), 39 far bottom left (Robyn Beck), 87 (Lester Cohen), 102 center left (Ron Galella, Ltd.), 70 left (Robin Lynne Gibson), 27 (Bruce Glikas/FilmMagic), 103 top left (Steve Granitz), 39 center left (Amy Graves), 39 bottom center, 49 (Mike Guastella), 39 center right (Frazer Harrison), 50, 51, 52, 102 bottom right, 103 bottom left (Mathew Imaging/FilmMagic), back cover, 20, 21, 38 (Jon Kopaloff/FilmMagic), 39 top right (Rob Loud), 41, 64 face (Jeffrey Mayer), 62 (Kevin Mazur), 39 top center, 56, 63, 80 (Jason Merritt/FilmMagic), cover, 92, 93, 99 (Frank Micelotta), 16 background (Michael Ochs Archives), 39 far center left (Jordan Strauss), 6 left, 39 bottom right (Noel Vasquez), 73, 84 (Kevin Winter); **Globe Photos:** 43 (Bruce Cotler), 77 (Nina Prommer), 24 (Barry Talesnick/IPOL); **Landov, LLC:** 97, 103 top right (Lucas Jackson/Reuters), 3, 65 (Kimberly P. Mitchell/MCT), 26 (Photopro), 2, 54, 96 (Aaron M. Sprecher/UPI), 42 (Roger Walsh); **London Features International Ltd.:** 76, 82 (David Longendyke), 91 top (Yuki Tanaka), 39 far center right, 64 hair, 102 top left (Dennis Van Tine), 39 far bottom right (Jacqui Wong); **NEWSCOM:** 18 (Anthony), 40 (Adriana M. Barraza/WENN), 30 (Disney/MCT), 7 right, 71, 78 (Infusla-62), 36 (KRT), 39 bottom left, 90 left (Byron Purvis/AdMedia), 89 (Brandon Todd/Splash News), 66 (WENN), 68, 81; **Retna Ltd.:** 55, 60 (Jay Blakesberg), 59 (Chris McAndrew/Camera Press), 17 (Harrison McClary), 12 (Mark Morrison), 7 center, 44, 103 bottom center (John Ricard), 7 left, 14, 35 foreground, 103 bottom right (Scott Weiner); **Reuters/Mario Anzuoni:** 74, 75; **ShutterStock, Inc.:** 15 (Tanya Kozlovsky), 70 right (Ronen); **WireImage.com:** 29 (Jeffrey Mayer), 88 bottom (Al Pereira).

Library of Congress Cataloging-in-Publication Data
Berne, Emma Carlson.
  Miley Cyrus / Emma Carlson Berne.
    p. cm. — (Junk food: tasty celebrity bios)
  Includes bibliographical references, discography, and index.
  Library/Book Clubs/Trade ISBN-10: 0-531-21722-1
  ISBN-13: 978-0-531-21722-1
  Book Fairs ISBN-10: 0-531-23402-9
  ISBN-13: 978-0-531-23402-0

  1. Cyrus, Miley, 1992—Juvenile literature. 2. Singers—United States—Biography—
Juvenile literature. 3. Actresses—United States—Biography—Juvenile literature. I. Title.
  ML3930.C98B47 2009   782.42164092—dc22   [B]   2008028314

1 2 3 4 5 6 7 8 9 10 R 18 17 16 15 14 16 12 11 10 09

JUNK ★ FOOD

TASTY CELEBRITY BIOS™

Miley
CYRUS

BY
EMMA CARLSON BERNE

Franklin Watts®
An Imprint of Scholastic Inc.

ONSTAGE
page 11

LARGER THAN LIFE:
Miley makes a big impression as Hannah Montana.

WiLL THE REaL miLeY CYRUS PLEaSe STanD UP?

Clutching your best friend's hand, you perch on the edge of your seat in a huge arena. The noise around you swells with anticipation as the stage lights flash on. You can hardly believe it. You're here, at a *Best of Both Worlds* concert, and you're about to see Hannah Montana.

Suddenly, a flash of light explodes onstage. You can hear yourself screaming with the rest of the crowd. A girl with

★ STAR ATTRACTION

MILEY'S *BEST OF BOTH WORLDS* TOUR was the hottest concert ticket of 2007. Miley was on the road for 106 days, and she performed in more than 60 cities.

ONSTAGE: Miley always started her concerts as Hannah.

long blond hair and sparkling pink tights appears in the center of the stage holding a microphone to her mouth. It's Hannah! You've seen her on TV a hundred times, and now she's right in front of you. But under the blond wig, there's a dark-haired teenage superstar waiting to appear.

Meet Miley Cyrus. For the *Best of Both Worlds* tour, Miley came out from behind her alter ego, Hannah. As it turns out, the real thing is every bit as cool as the TV character. And the story of her journey from Tennessee farm girl to pop phenom is just as fascinating.

WHOA! Little Miley sits tall on one of the family's horses.

BORN in THE SPOTLiGHT

Miley grew up on a Tennessee farm, but she was destined for the stage from the start.

Destiny Hope Cyrus smiled all the time when she was a baby. She smiled so much that her mom and dad started calling her "Smiley." Pretty soon, "Smiley" turned into "Miley." Hardly anyone except her grandmother called her "Destiny Hope" ever again. Chances are no one ever will, now that cheerful little "Miley" has become one of the

DADDY'S GIRL: Miley, almost two years old, with her famous dad, Billy Ray Cyrus.

DiD YOU KNOW?

MILEY MAKES MILLIONS OF DOLLARS A YEAR. But her parents still give her a $300-a-month allowance!

most popular TV and music stars in the world.

Miley's dad is country singer Billy Ray Cyrus. In 1992, he had one of the hottest country songs on the charts, "Achy-Breaky Heart." An overnight sensation, Billy Ray moved to Singing Hills, a 500-acre farm in a little town called Thompson's Station. That's near Nashville, Tennessee. He married a woman with long blond hair and a beautiful smile named Leticia "Tish" Finley. And on November 23, 1992, Destiny Hope was born.

DOWN ON THE FARM

Miley grew up with lots of brothers and sisters to play with. Tish brought two children, Trace and Brandi, into the marriage. Billy Ray already had a son named Christopher Cody. And before long, Miley had two more siblings: a little brother, Braison, and a little sister, Noah Lindsey.

The Cyrus farm was a fun place for a kid. There were plenty of horses and other animals. Sometimes, Miley and her dad would spend all day exploring the farm. Billy Ray had mowed miles of paths with his tractor. Other times, they'd saddle up the horses and ride through the rolling hills.

As much as she loved the quiet times on the farm, Miley was a performer from

HORSE LOVER: There were seven horses on the Cyrus farm. Miley loved to braid their tails.

the start. She was her daddy's girl, and just like Billy Ray, she was drawn to the spotlight. "[When] I was little," Miley told *USA Today*, "I would stand up on couches and say, 'Watch me . . .'"

When Miley was little, Billy Ray spent a lot of time on tour. Often, the whole Cyrus family packed up and went with him. Whenever she could, Miley stood in the wings and watched her dad perform.

MILEY TAKES THE STAGE

One night, Miley was backstage with her nanny when she decided she didn't want to watch from the sidelines anymore. Onstage, her dad was singing Elvis songs with a band full of country-music stars. "[There] were all these people there—legends, everyone," Miley told *ABC News*. Miley couldn't stand it any longer. She kicked her way free from her nanny and ran out onstage before anyone could catch her. Little Miley grabbed a microphone. Then, in

ELVIS ROCKS: Miley made Elvis Presley songs her trademark.

IN THE WINGS: Miley, age eight, waits for her turn at the mike.

front of an auditorium full of people, she started singing.

From the start, Miley was a huge hit. Her dad realized he had a good thing going and made Miley a regular part of his act. Elvis songs were her trademark. "She'd come out and sing 'Hound Dog,' and the crowd would just go crazy," Billy Ray told *The Early Show*.

For Miley, it was love at first sight—with the stage!

ALL-STAR CHEERLEADER

When she wasn't on tour with her dad, Miley went to public school in the nearby town of Franklin. She attended church with her family every Sunday.

Miley also got involved in competitive cheerleading. Her

MAMA'S GIRL, TOO: Billy Ray and Miley are tight. But Miley and her mom, Tish, are really close as well.

squad, the Premier Tennessee All Stars, traveled to competitions all around the state. The hard work didn't bother Miley a bit. "The training is pretty harsh," she said during an interview with the *Philadelphia Inquirer*, "but it's so worth it once you're onstage and getting trophies."

When Miley was about nine, Billy Ray landed the lead role on a PAX cable show called *Doc*. He was cast as a country doctor who moves to a big city. The only catch was that the series was filming in Toronto. Billy Ray had to leave his family behind and move to Canada.

It was hard for Miley to have her dad a thousand miles away. But she and the rest of the family visited Billy Ray whenever they could—and his new job turned out to have a silver lining. Watching her dad on the set of *Doc*, Miley began to think that maybe *she* could be an actor too.

UPS and DOWNS

With her dad as inspiration, Miley started taking private acting lessons and studying with a coach. Her dedication amazed her family. Billy Ray said on ABC's *20/20*, "I've never seen anybody that driven . . . to be like, 'I'm gonna be a great actress, Daddy.' Kids would be out playing and ice-skating, building a snowman. Miley would be in a theater studying with a coach."

Miley started going to auditions, looking for small parts in movies and TV series. She was cast with her dad in three episodes of *Doc*, and she got a small part in the Tim Burton movie *Big Fish*.

But like any aspiring actor, Miley also got plenty of rejections. It was hard for her family to see her hurting. Billy Ray told *People*, "I'd see those little tears

MILEY EXPOSED!

One of Miley's all-time most embarrassing moments was when she ripped her jean skirt while practicing for dance team tryouts. She slipped and tore it right in front of all the kids in the hallway. Even more mortifying: The guidance counselor called Miley's mom to bring her a new outfit!

come down her face, and I'd hold her and say, 'Enjoy being a kid. [Don't let this] mess up your childhood.'"

Billy Ray and Tish never pushed Miley to perform. In fact, they encouraged her to have fun and relax. "I would say, 'Hey, why don't you just be a kid for a while, enjoy school, enjoy cheerleading, take some time off from auditions?'" Billy Ray told the *New York Daily News*. "She wouldn't hear of that. She was always very serious."

It's a good thing that Miley was so determined to succeed. Thousands of miles away, in Los Angeles, California, Disney producers were dreaming up a TV series about an ordinary girl who leads a double life as a rock star. They just needed to find the right actress for the title role.

T or F

?

Miley is scared of dogs.

FALSE!
Miley loves animals.
She has three dogs: Loco,
Juicy, and Minnie Pearl.

ALWAYS MILEY: "Even though I change the way I look, I don't change my personality," Miley says.

miLEY'S moment

Disney says she's too young to be Hannah— but Miley won't take no for an answer.

In Tennessee, Miley heard that Disney was auditioning actresses for a new TV series. The show was based on an episode from the series *That's So Raven*, in which a child TV star decides to go to a normal high school. The producers were calling the main character Zoe Stewart, and her stage name was Alexis Texas. They thought they had a potential hit—maybe something as big as *Lizzie McGuire*, with Hilary Duff. But first they had to find the perfect girl for the lead role. "We said we will not

IN THE BIG APPLE: Miley is photographed in New York City in the summer of 2007.

go forward until we can find an actress who can carry a sitcom as well as she can carry a tune," said Gary Marsh from Disney, in an interview with the *Philadelphia Inquirer*.

DID YOU KNOW?

EARLY NAMES FOR THE HANNAH CHARACTER included **Alexis Texas, Anna Cabana, and Samantha York.**

At the time, no one thought Miley fit that description. She didn't have much acting experience. And at 11, she was still way too young. The producers were looking for a 15- or 16-year-old to play the lead.

The odds were against her, but true to form, Miley decided to go for it. She sent an audition tape to Disney.

Miley's tape arrived in Hollywood and went into a stack of hundreds. When the producers got around to her, they were intrigued. They loved Miley's infectious smile, her energy, and her voice. But they couldn't see her in the lead role. Miley looked young and her front teeth were still growing in. She was, they said, "too small."

As usual, Miley didn't let the rejection stop her. She kept working on her acting. She took more lessons. And when she turned 12, she sent in *another* tape. Once again, the producers loved her but thought she was too young.

WOWiNG DiSNeY

A lot of girls might have given up at this point. But, as Miley told the *London Times*, her dad's advice kept her going: "If there's a will there's a way," he often said. "It's about getting what you want done and having a great time while you're doing it." Miley knew she was perfect for the show. She just had to figure out how to convince Disney.

Miley had her agent call the producers and ask whether she could fly to Burbank, California, where the auditions for the show were taking place. Rarely do actors do that. Usually, they wait for a studio to fly them in.

At the studio, Miley faced a room full of

GOING HOLLYWOOD:
Miley at the premiere of *High School Musical* in 2006.

producers, Disney executives, and camera operators. By this time, the Alexis Texas character was called Hannah Montana. The producers wanted Miley to read part of the script for the cameras. Miley took a deep breath—this was the moment she'd been waiting for. She read the parts of both Hannah and Lilly, Hannah's best friend.

The Disney execs found that in person, it was Miley's charisma and talent that came through, not her age. "We saw a girl who has this natural ebullience," Marsh told *USA Today*. "She loves every minute of her life."

Miley has braces.

TRUE!
Her orthodontist put them on the insides of her teeth so that you can't see them!

miLey = Hannah

Miley sang for the producers; she read more scenes; she chatted about life back home. Marsh thought that Miley was a combination of Hilary Duff and Shania Twain. She was someone girls could relate to, like Hilary, and she had a big stage presence, like Shania. The producers had Miley come back for one final audition. Then they made up their minds: The search was over. Miley Cyrus was now . . . *Hannah Montana*!

It's easy to imagine Miley jumping up and down and screaming when Disney called with the news. Her family was ecstatic. "I don't mean to sound like too much of a proud papa," Billy Ray said to a *New York Daily News* reporter, "but she is amazing."

BiLLY RaY = ROBBie

The producers now had to choose someone to play Robbie, Miley's dad and manager on the show. In the age of reality TV, Billy Ray seemed like a natural.

Billy Ray wasn't so sure. He recalled his concerns for the *Daily News*. "This is Miley's thing," he remembered thinking. "She's worked too hard on it. . . . I didn't want to come in and mess up her show."

Miley encouraged her dad to try. Billy Ray was nervous when he went in for the audition. But he had been performing for a long time, and so he knew what to do. He played his guitar and sang a duet with Miley. They read some scenes together. They showed the producers their special, super-complicated handshake. Basically, they acted the way they usually did at home—like buds.

DETERMINED: Miley's dad says, "I've seen her go to so many auditions and be turned away and just keep on keeping on."

TRUE PALS: "I feel like I can tell my dad anything," Miley says.

The producers auditioned a few other actors, but they kept coming back to Billy Ray. He and Miley had a great relationship, both on camera and off. Everyone could see how much they cared about each other. Eventually, they decided: Billy Ray was hired!

Miley and her dad couldn't believe how lucky they were. "We just found the right show at the right time, and we were both in the right spaces of our lives for this whole thing," Billy Ray told the *Washington Post*. "It's a moment in time."

It has turned out to be a pretty long moment.

DiD YOU KnOW?

MILEY GOT HER FIRST GUITAR WHEN SHE WAS 12.

The company Daisy Rock makes guitars especially for girls and women. When Miley was 12, they asked her to be their spokesperson and gave her a free guitar! It was a Stardust Acoustic/Electric.

a long way from Tennessee

Miley goes from country girl to Hollywood superstar— all in a few months.

Miley's dedication had landed her the role of a lifetime. But the hard work was just beginning, and it soon became clear that Miley's life was about to change forever.

Billy Ray knew what was happening. He was thrilled for Miley, but he also felt sad that his girl was about to grow up so quickly. After Miley got the part, he wrote a song called

"Ready, Set, Don't Go." Billy Ray told ABC's *20/20* that the song is "about that moment in every parent's life when you realize that your child is growing up. And you're at that crossroad where you have to let them go."

Miley's new life meant big changes for the entire family. The family would have to move to California, where *Hannah Montana* was being filmed. Their 500 acres of farmland were about to be exchanged for a suburban backyard.

Miley said good-bye to her school, her friends, and her horses. She and her family packed up their stuff—and moved to Los Angeles.

Miley missed the farm and her friends, but she didn't have much time to feel homesick. As soon as she got settled, she started shooting the first season of *Hannah*. That meant an entirely new schedule. Every day, she got up at 7:15. Her

LOOSE LIPS! Miley tells her mom *everything*. Once, she told Tish a secret about a guy her friend liked. Later, when Miley's friend came over, Miley's mom totally spilled! She told Miley's friend that she knew the guy's mother and could introduce them whenever she wanted!

side by side

MiLEY CYRUS

HaҗҗaH MONTana

	MiLEY CYRUS	HaҗҗaH MONTana
Hair color	Brown	Blond
Solo albums	*Hannah Montana 2: Meet Miley Cyrus*	*Hannah Montana*
	Breakout	*Hannah Montana 2: Meet Miley Cyrus*
		Hannah Montana 2: Non-Stop Dance Party
Personal style	Princess meets rocker chick	Colorful and trendy
Musical sound	Mixed and edgy	Danceable pop music
Backup dancers?	No	Yes

GET IT STRAIGHT: On *Hannah Montana*, Miley Cyrus plays the part of Miley Stewart, who is *also* the pop star Hannah Montana. Her best friend on the show is Lilly Truscott, played by Emily Osment.

ON THE SET OF *HANNAH MONTANA*

EMILY OSMENT
aka Lilly Truscott

BORN: March 10, 1992, in Los Angeles, CA

ROLE ON *HANNAH*: Best friend

OLDER BROTHER: Actor Haley Joel Osment

FAVORITE HOBBIES: Writing, playing golf, knitting

FAVORITE MOVIE: *Breakfast at Tiffany's*

FAVORITE TV CHANNEL: Turner Classic Movies

FAVORITE SPORT: Soccer

FAST FACT: Her parents wouldn't let her see her big brother's movie *The Sixth Sense* because they thought she was too young!

SONGS RECORDED: "I Don't Think About It," on *I Don't Think About It*; "You've Got a Friend," (with Billy Ray Cyrus) on *Home at Last*; "If I Didn't Have You," with Mitchel Musso; "Strangers Like Me," with the Disney Channel Circle of Stars on the *Tarzan* DVD

dad made her a hot cup of Ovaltine, and they hopped in their chauffeured SUV to get to the studio by 8:30. Miley usually spent eight or nine hours a day on the set.

DOING IT ALL

Somehow, Miley found the time to get an education. But while Hannah Montana goes to a regular school, Miley had to get creative about her classes. Her parents hired a tutor to give her lessons for three hours every day on the set. On

Fridays, she went to a school called Options for Youth, where she did more work and took all her exams. Options for Youth is a charter school that offers students an alternative to traditional classes.

Adjusting to the new routine wasn't always easy for Miley and her dad. Sometimes the pressure of working together led to fights. Miley told *Blast* magazine that she once kept her dad waiting for an hour at the end of the day while she redid her makeup. Billy Ray was not happy.

It wasn't long, though, before Miley realized that she loved working with her dad. "We're really close," she said during an interview with *People*. "I feel like I can tell my dad anything. When we come home, we forget that we even work together, and we just hang out."

Billy Ray, too, seemed to love working with his daughter. Despite the way he felt when he wrote "Ready, Set, Don't Go," their new life was actually bringing them

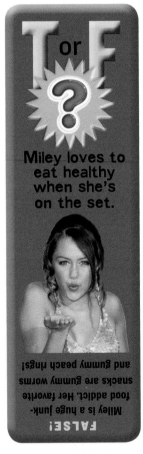

T or F ?

Miley loves to eat healthy when she's on the set.

FALSE! Miley is a huge junk-food addict. Her favorite snacks are gummy worms and gummy peach rings!

miLeY & FRieNDS

GUEST STARS ON *HANNAH*

ASHLEY TISDALE as Maddie Fitzpatrick in the episode "On the Road Again"

HEATHER LOCKLEAR as Heather Truscott in "Lilly's Mom Has Got It Goin' On"

RAVEN-SYMONÉ as Raven Baxter in "That's So Suite Life of Hannah Montana"

JOEY FATONE as Joey Vitolo in "Bye Bye Ball"

CORBIN BLEU as Johnny Collins in "Lilly, Do You Want to Know a Secret?"

THE JONAS BROTHERS as themselves in "Me and Mr. Jonas and Mr. Jonas and Mr. Jonas"

DOLLY PARTON as Aunt Dolly in "Good Golly, Miss Dolly"

JESSE MCCARTNEY as himself in "When You Wish You Were the Star"

COLE and **DYLAN SPROUSE** as Cody and Zack Martin in "That's So Suite Life of Hannah Montana"

NOAH LINDSAY CYRUS as the Little Girl in "O Say, Can You Remember the Words?"

SELENA GOMEZ as Mikayla in "I Want You to Want Me . . . to Go to Florida"

closer. "We get to spend a lot of time with each other, which I consider a major plus because life goes by so fast," Billy Ray told the *Washington Post*.

new Best Buds

Miley's dad wasn't the only person around to help her make the transition to Hollywood. Miley also became good friends with her co-stars. Jason Earles, for one, was impressed by how sweet Miley was in person. "She could be awful if she wanted to," he told *USA Today*. "But she's not. She's about as sweet a person as you could want."

on THe seT
OF Hannah montana

JASON EARLES
aka Jackson Stewart

BORN: April 26, 19?? in San Diego, CA (No one can figure out what year Jason was born. Some articles report that he was born in 1977. But Jason's own resume says that he was born in 1985!)

ROLE ON HANNAH: Older brother

FAVORITE ANIMALS: Horses and cheetahs

FAVORITE MUSIC: Alternative

FAVORITE COLOR: Blue

FAST FACT: Jason is a really good cook and likes to make BBQ.

Jason is older than Miley and he's a trained Shakespearean actor, so he's probably had some acting tricks to share. He's also been in a bunch of other movies, like *National Treasure* with Nicholas Cage, and *American Pie Presents: Band Camp*.

Miley also got a lot of support from Emily Osment and Mitchel Musso, who play her onscreen buds Lilly and Oliver. Emily comes from a Hollywood family. Her dad is an actor and her older brother is Haley Joel Osment, who starred in *The Sixth Sense*. Emily's been acting since she was six, when she appeared in an ad for flowers. Her best-known part before *Hannah Montana* was Gerti Giggles in two of the *Spy Kids* movies. But even though she's so show-biz savvy, Emily was completely psyched to get the part in *Hannah*. She told *USA Today* that she "screamed for ten minutes" when she got the part. "I knew the show would go far," she added, "but not this far."

When Mitchel landed the part of Oliver, he hadn't had as much experience as Emily. But he had been in a movie called *Secondhand*

GOOD VIBES: Miley and her *Hannah* co-stars were friends from day one.

Lions, with Emily's big brother, Haley Joel. And he'd already worked with Disney. Mitchell played Raymond Figg in a Disney Channel movie called *Life Is Ruff*.

OVERNIGHT SENSATION

With her new friends and her dad by her side, Miley got ready for the big day: March 24, 2006, the *Hannah Montana* premiere. Michael Poryes, the series executive producer, told the *New York Daily News*, "[I] remember actually sitting down with Miley and the other kids . . . and telling them,

'Your lives are going to be forever different.'"

Poryes was right. The show was an instant sensation. The day after the premiere, Miley went to the Universal Studios amusement park with her brother and a friend. "The recognition was immediate," she said to the *Philadelphia Inquirer*. "It was craziness—all the kids on every ride. I felt like I was going to hurl after one ride and all the kids were like, 'Hannah Montana is about to puke!'"

Before anyone could blink, *Hannah* was the number one cable show for kids aged six to 14. Miley and her cast mates were having the time of their lives. "It's so awesome," Miley told the *New York Daily News*. "I've never really done anything like this before. I really like it because it's natural. I don't really have to act too much. . . . It's definitely something a lot of girls my age would love to do because who wouldn't want to be a rock star?"

PEACE! On a trip to New York City, Miley signals to photographers from the back of a limo.

43

LOVE, MILEY: The star signs her CD, *Hannah Montana 2: Meet Miley Cyrus*, released in 2007.

rolled from city to city, people began to notice something. Often, before the shows began, the fans chanted just as loudly for Miley.

NUMBER ONE

The fall passed in a blur of cheering crowds and long bus rides. By late October, Miley was back in L.A., working on the next season of *Hannah*. That month, the sound-track from the show, *Hannah Montana: Songs From and Inspired by the Hit TV Series*, was released. Everyone thought it would sell well, but even Disney was probably surprised when the album became the first TV soundtrack to enter the Billboard Top 200 at number one. By January 2007, the *Hannah Montana* album had sold two million copies.

Now the music industry was starting to take a good look at this girl from Tennessee. It was obvious that Miley

> Miley has accomplished more than most artists who've been in the business for 20 years.
>
> **RYAN SEACREST**
> to *US Weekly*

was not just a cute sitcom actress. She was a real musician. Before long, Hollywood Records offered Miley a four-album deal to record some of her own songs.

SOOO BUSY!

Touring, signing with record companies, taping the show—Miley's life was insane. But somehow she found time for a little romance. Miley has said that her dating life can get complicated. "I try [to date]," she told the *Early Show*. "It doesn't work too well,

STAR STATS
NICK JONAS

BORN: September 16, 1992

SIGN: Virgo

HEIGHT: 5´6˝

FAST FACT: Nick has Type I diabetes, so he has to keep careful track of his blood sugar and insulin levels while on tour.

STAR STATS
JOE JONAS

BORN: August 15, 1989

SIGN: Leo

HEIGHT: 5´8˝

FAST FACT: Before he was a musician, Joe wanted to do stand-up and sketch comedy.

because I'll have a boyfriend for, like, a day, and OK, you can never call me because [I'm] always working. So that gets difficult. I think my dad likes the job because it keeps the boys away. But [there are some] really cute guest stars."

miley ♡ nick?

One of those cute guests happened to be Nick Jonas, the youngest member of the super-hot boy group, the Jonas Brothers. Nick appeared on *Hannah* in August 2007, along with his brothers Kevin and Joe. The Jonases are from New Jersey. They've always loved singing and performing. Nick has even been on Broadway. Since 2005, the dark-eyed trio has been recording albums and touring, often with Disney stars like Aly & AJ, and The Cheetah Girls. Sometime during the summer of 2007, Miley and Nick started dating. They didn't reveal much about their relationship, but one thing is for sure: Miley had to keep it low-key. Billy Ray and Tish have said that Miley hasn't gone on a *real* date yet. "What the kids do these days is they have group dates," Billy Ray told *People*. "A whole bunch of kids go to a movie or to a pizza joint."

After dating for a while, Miley and Nick broke up. Maybe they weren't right for each other. Or maybe their schedules just made it hard to spend time together. But the two stars remain really good friends—and *maybe* something more. After all, Nick did tell *People* magazine: "We're good friends. We'll see what happens. Maybe there's a relationship there one day." Keep dreaming, Nick!

A WILD RIDE: Nick and Miley found time to visit Six Flags in 2007.

side by side

Album title	Hannah Montana: Songs From and Inspired by the Hit TV Series	Hannah Montana 2: Meet Miley Cyrus (double disc)
Release date	October 24, 2006	June 26, 2007
Length	43 minutes	Disc 1: 35 minutes Disc 2: 33 minutes
Number of weeks at number one on the *Billboard* charts	2	1
Certification	multi-platinum	multi-platinum

BiRTHDaY GiRL

There was plenty more excitement for Miley in 2007. The second *Hannah* soundtrack debuted and eventually went double platinum. Miley wrapped filming on the second season of the show. She even made an appearance on *Oprah*. But the highlight of the year was definitely Miley's fifteenth birthday in November. Two days before Miley's actual birthday on November 21, Tish threw her a hometown surprise party with a 1980s theme. She took Miley to a club in Franklin. Miley thought she

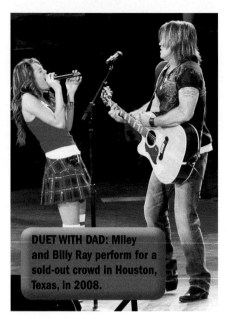

DUET WITH DAD: Miley and Billy Ray perform for a sold-out crowd in Houston, Texas, in 2008.

was going to see one of her favorite bands, Paramore. But she was shocked to find out that her mother had more than that up her sleeve. "I go in and every one of my friends from like second grade was there!" Miley told *People*.

That wasn't the end of the celebration. Two nights later, on her actual birthday, Miley performed for 15,000 fans in Nashville. At the end of the concert, the audience sang "Happy Birthday," a cake arrived onstage, and a major fireworks display exploded overhead. The Jonas Brothers presented her with 15 roses in front of the audience, and Miley got to sing a duet with her dad.

Fifteen was fun, but Miley had already told *US Weekly* what she wanted for her *sixteenth* birthday: a customized 1950s Corvette. "I want black with three white stripes, black interior, red rearview mirror, and red stitching on the seats. With my initials on it!"

GOOD NIGHT, EVERYBODY!
Nick Jonas, Miley, and Kevin
Jonas thank their fans.

LIVE IN CONCERT: In 2007, Miley took her show on the road with the *Best of Both Worlds* tour.

Fans get the "Best of Both Worlds" in Miley's new show—if they can find a ticket!

By the time Miley turned 15, her name—and Hannah's—were fast becoming household words all across the country. Disney knew they had more than just a popular star on their hands. They had a phenomenon. For Miley, there would be no more opening for other bands. Disney was sending her out on her own tour. And this time, Miley would perform half the concert as Hannah, and half as *herself*—Miley Cyrus. Now she could show her fans that she was more than just Hannah Montana.

A major concert tour is a huge production. In the summer of 2007, the wheels turned fast and furiously. Miley worked under veteran director Kenny Ortega to put all the pieces together. Kenny hired lighting designers, choreographers, backup singers and dancers, stage managers, costume designers, seamstresses, stagehands, and sound engineers.

PUTTiNG iT TOGETHER

The director controls the general look and feel of a concert, and Kenny, who had worked in Hollywood since the 1980s, was the perfect man for the job. He did the choreography for *Dirty Dancing*, Madonna's "Material Girl" video, *The Cheetah Girls 2,* and the two *High School Musical* movies. He was also the guy behind the 2002 Winter Olympics Opening Ceremony in Salt Lake City, Utah.

DiD YOU KNOW?

MILEY HAS DONE SOMETHING THAT NEITHER THE BEATLES NOR ELVIS COULD DO.

She had *seven* singles on the Billboard charts at the same time!

With Kenny's direction—and Miley's input—the show started to come together. Miley says she was inspired by big classic rock bands like U2 and the Rolling Stones. The stage, for instance, was designed with a ramp extending out into the audience so Miley could dance into the crowd the way Mick Jagger loves to do.

For an opening band, Miley scored the Jonas Brothers.

PRACTICE, PRACTICE: Miley worked hard to perfect her dance moves for the tour.

The brothers would come out first and do their own songs and then reappear to perform a few tunes with Miley. Their slightly edgier sound was a great contrast to Miley's sweet pop tunes.

In the fall, Miley devoted herself to rehearsals. Every day, Kenny helped her run through her dance steps with her backup dancers and singers. Miley and her backups made sure they were in time with the band and with each other. Miley also had to practice her costume changes, some of which left her with only a minute to put on a whole different outfit.

meet miley cyrus

Finally, on October 18, 2007, in St. Louis, Missouri, the big night arrived. It's easy to imagine Miley standing backstage, a few butterflies in her stomach as she waits for the Jonases to finish their performance. Then she bursts onstage in a blaze of colored lights. The crowd screams, waving their arms. "We have a couple of rules here tonight," Miley told the fans each night. "I don't want to look around and see anyone sitting in their seats."

No problem—Miley had thousands of people on their feet for every two-hour show.

Miley started each performance as Hannah,

BEST OF BOTH WORLDS:
Joe Jonas sings with Miley
(performing as Hannah) during
Miley's smash 2007 tour.

surrounded by dancers wearing brightly colored, coordinated outfits. She ran up and down the long stage ramp in her blond wig, belting out her tunes and reaching into the crowd to touch people's hands. As Hannah, Miley's outfits were colorful and trendy, with plenty of pink and sparkles. Her dances were elaborate; at one point, some of her male backup dancers threw her high in the air.

Midway through the performance, Miley transformed into herself. She disappeared for a moment and then came back with her own long dark hair flowing down her back. She ditched the pink for denim and t-shirts. One Miley outfit included a biker vest and a chain around her waist. Like her outfits, Miley's own songs are a little edgier than Hannah's—more rock and less pop. Miley even tried a

HAIR-RAISING! Once, while Miley was performing onstage, one of her dancers' rings got caught in her wig. He and Miley had to keep dancing while his hand was stuck to her head. Finally, he managed to rip his hand free, but he took a lot of hair with it. Luckily, her wig stayed on!

few Mick Jagger moves she had seen on a concert video. "[Mick] did this really cool slide, and I tried to do it, but got caught underneath a Plexiglas sheet [onstage]. I cut my knee open," Miley told Canada's *Globe and Mail* newspaper.

WiSH YOU WeRe HeRe

Life on the road was a strain for Miley, as it is for most performers. Most of the time, she did fine. She had her essentials with her: her Killers CD, her iPod, a travel Bible, and her hair straightener. Her mom, sisters, and grandmother traveled with her, and her uncle Mick filled in as her tour manager and bodyguard. But Billy Ray stayed at home to take care of the rest of the kids, and Miley really missed him. She told *People* magazine, "I look forward to when I go back to [taping] *Hannah Montana* because what I really miss is being with him 24/7." Luckily, they found a way to keep in touch: Billy Ray sang to Miley over video chat.

TOP CHOICE:
Miley performs at Nickelodeon's 2008 Kids' Choice Awards.

FLATTERED AND FREAKED OUT

The tour was a giant success. By December, Miley added another 14 concerts, starting in Detroit and ending in Miami. Even so, the shows sold out instantly. In many cases, tickets were gone five minutes after they went on sale online. All over the country, people did extreme things to get access to Miley's shows. One radio station invited dads to compete in a race for tickets; the only catch was, they had to run in high heels!

Miley wasn't sure whether to be flattered or freaked out by the attention. "Having so many people after the tickets and so many people wanting to come, it shows how many people really support you, and that's good to hear," she told the *Globe and Mail*. But at times the clamor for tickets got out of control.

The desperate attempts to get Miley tickets shed light on a big problem in the entertainment

T or F

Miley's Hannah Montana wig was once worn by model Cindy Crawford.

FALSE! Miley's Hannah Montana wigs are custom-made for her, and she has four of them.

HANNAH WANNABES: A few young fans in Michigan pose in Hannah wigs.

business. Popular shows of all kinds—not just Miley's—often sell out at normal prices within minutes after tickets go on sale. That's because companies known as ticket brokers buy up all the tickets online. Then the brokers resell them at outrageous prices—sometimes for as much as $2,000!

Brokers had been selling tickets like this for years, but the issue didn't boil over until Miley's fans got mad. Now, in the midst of her wildly popular tour, Miley found herself at the center of a major legal battle.

NOWHERE TO HIDE: Miley is surrounded by the press as she goes shopping in L.A.

THE WORLD iS WATCHING

In the glare of the spotlight, Miley looks for a place to hide.

By the middle of the *Best of Both Worlds* tour, problems were piling up for Miley. She was beginning to realize that fame can have a serious downside. First of all, the ticket situation was making national news. Outside companies called ticket brokers were accused of buying up tickets to Miley's concerts and reselling them at much higher prices. These brokers were not affiliated with Miley or Disney, and Miley felt bad for her fans. "I hated it that people were being taken advantage of," she told *Us Weekly*.

DiD YOU KnOW?

MILEY HAS THE WEIRD AL YANKOVIC SONG
"White and Nerdy" on her iPod!

SHE'S MAGIC: Miley appears at the opening for *Harry Potter and the Order of the Phoenix* in Hollywood in 2007.

DOUBLE TROUBLE

Controversy even followed Miley onto the stage. In 2008, someone posted a video on the website YouTube showing Miley using a body double during a *Best of Both Worlds* performance. Dressed as Hannah, Miley ducks offstage through a side door during the song "We Got the Party." Immediately, another girl dressed in the same clothes, with a long blond wig partly covering her face, enters and starts dancing and lip-synching to the music. She stays at the back of the stage where her face can't easily be seen.

QUICK—SWITCH!

The video created enough of a flap that Miley had to explain the mysterious Hannah double. Miley pointed out that on the TV show, her Hannah-to-Miley transition takes an hour and a half with costume, hair, and makeup. Onstage, she only had a minute and 50 seconds to make the switch. Since she really needed at least three or four minutes, the production team decided to use a double. The body double was onstage for only one or two minutes. But since people were upset by the switch, Miley and her crew changed the song order so that they didn't have to use the double at all.

T or F

?

Miley's mom once took away her cell phone when Miley refused to change out of a shirt that showed her belly.

Tish is very strict about what Miley wears.

TRUE!

The body double issue seemed like a small one, but Miley had reached the height of fame, and she had people watching every move she made. At times, the scrutiny drove her crazy. Miley can barely go out to dinner or ride her bike without attracting a crowd. Once, she was shopping in a mall with a friend when they turned around to find 50 people following them. When she browses for clothes, fans recognize her and flood the store. "Managers and everyone hate me," Miley told *USA Today*. "They're like, 'Please get out of the store,' because it gets so insane. It's pretty crazy."

Miley and her family have tried hard to preserve at least some privacy. Miley sometimes wears wigs and sunglasses, but they never work. The Cyruses have even moved three times in two years because fans keep coming to the door and ringing the doorbell. "Being famous is like a dream come true," Miley told *People*. "But it's really difficult because you lose your freedom."

ALL EYES ON MILEY

With fans everywhere, Miley needs to be "on" all the time, even when she's tired or doesn't feel like talking. She can't snicker when fans ask her weird questions, like what her favorite kind of cheese is, or what her blood type is. "I think that's the hardest part," she said on *ABC News*, "keeping up your energy and making sure you can really relate to all the people that you're going to meet."

POOCH PATROL: Partially hidden by a hat and sunglasses, Miley takes to the streets to look for her aunt's lost dog.

CAN I HAVE YOUR AUTOGRAPH? Fans swarm around Miley at the Kids' Choice Awards in 2008.

Sometimes, the stress of public life catches up with Miley. She has high expectations for herself and worries that she'll disappoint all the people who depend on her. What if her fans get tired of her? she wonders. What if her albums don't sell? Miley told *People* that she knows how fast she could fall. "It's a long ride to the top, but it's only a short ride down. So it makes me really nervous. I'm like, 'Oh my gosh, am I doing enough? Are people still into my music?' I get stressed out."

"THIS IS THE LIFE"

Miley's family has always told her she could drop it all and go back to a normal childhood. Billy Ray likes to remind Miley that anytime she wants, they can leave Hollywood and return to Tennessee. All her horses are still waiting for her there on the farm, he says.

But for Miley, there's no turning back.

THE FAVORITE: Miley won "Favorite TV Actress" AND "Favorite Female Singer" at Nickelodeon's 2008 Kids' Choice Awards.

KEEPiNG iT ReaL

Can a megastar like Miley live the life of a normal teenager? At least she can try.

The days of long, quiet horseback rides through the Tennessee farm are gone for Miley—at least for now. But she finds ways to keep herself grounded even while her career climbs to dizzying heights.

You could say that in some ways Miley combines the best of two worlds. "What's amazing about Miley," Disney's Gary Marsh told the *Philadelphia Inquirer,* "is she's very natural but completely

75

self-aware. She's precocious but a complete innocent. It's a unique combination that enables her to straddle two worlds as she plays Miley and Hannah." It also helps her manage the two sides of her real life—the Hollywood Miley and the Tennessee Miley.

> She'll really back you up. . . . She'll stand up for you—that's what I love about Miley.
>
> **EMILY OSMENT**
> *Hannah Montana* co-star

MiLEY DOES CHORES?!

Miley's family is the biggest source of stability in her frenetic life. Her parents try never to add to the pressure Miley puts on herself. Moving back to Tennessee is always a real option. And, as Tish told *People*, "[Miley] knows that if there was any time I felt like things were getting to be too much for her, we would just not do it."

Both Tish and Billy Ray make sure Miley finds time in her crazy schedule for the activities of an

OVERHEARD!

HOLD ON! Fame has been a wild ride for Miley and her family.

average teenager. "We try to make it as normal as possible living in this world that she's in," Billy Ray told *People* magazine.

In part, that means that when Miley isn't touring, taping the TV show, recording music, or making public appearances for Disney—she has to do chores! She loads the dishwasher, keeps her room clean, and folds laundry. Unfortunately, Miley's not very *good* at her chores. Once, when she was trying to figure out the new dishwasher, she added way too much soap. When she turned it on, it flooded the floor with bubbles. Another time, she shrank

MILEY AND MOM:
Tish always has
Miley's back.

her mom's favorite jeans in the dryer. "In our family, because our legs are so long, we're not supposed to put jeans in the dryer because they'll shrink up," Miley told *Blast*. "We have to hang them outside to dry the old-fashioned way. Now [my mom's] got really cute capris!"

SCHOOL RULES

Miley does better at schoolwork than she does at her chores—lucky for her, since she's expected to take it seriously no matter how tough her professional life gets. Miley says her teachers at Options for Youth are just as hard on her as they are on everyone else. "My shooting schedule is easy compared to what I do at school," she told *Blast*. "This was the rule, that acting and singing is my 'side stuff.' If you came to my school, you'd see a whole different side of me. There I'm like, 'OK, it's time to get down and study.'"

TEACHER'S PET: Miley visits with a former teacher, Nancy Sevier, who surprised the star with some of her artwork from second grade.

Miley's taking all the same classes that any high-schooler would take. Math and history are not her favorites, but she loves creative writing. Miley's even writing a book of her own. She told *Newsweek* it's called *The Diary of Priscilla's Coffeehouse*. "[It's] about all the people I met at this coffee shop," Miley said. "I don't want to publish it or anything. It's a book for myself."

CLOTHES HORSE

Of course, Miley doesn't work *all* the time. Every day after taping, she and her mom go shopping—especially for shoes. Miley loves changing her style. "Sometimes I'll be punky, the next day I'll be preppy," Miley told *USA Today*. When she's home and not on the road, Miley and her brother Braison ride their bikes together every day after breakfast. The Cyruses throw barbecues for all their neighbors on the street.

T or F

?

Miley's natural hair color is blond. The producers of *Hannah Montana* made her dye it brown for the show.

FALSE!
Miley is a natural brunette.

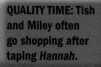

QUALITY TIME: Tish and Miley often go shopping after taping *Hannah*.

MILEY'S WORLD

Billy Ray and Tish want to keep Miley in this world of shopping trips, bike rides, and barbecues for as long as they can. They recently got Miley to promise she would live at home until she's 20 years old. To sweeten the deal, they built a new wing on their house in L.A., just for Miley. It has a bedroom, a living room, and a separate entrance. Most of the time though, Tish keeps that entrance locked!

Miley's friends give her another way to escape from the pressures of fame. Miley and her *Hannah* co-stars, Emily Osment and Mitchel Musso, are really tight. Even when they've spent all day on the set together, they text each other and have conference calls almost every night. Miley showed Emily how to play guitar, and Emily showed Miley how to knit. "[Emily and I] are complete opposites, and sometimes we don't agree," Miley told the *Australia Sunday Mail*. "She's very into soccer, and I'm more of a shopper. But our friendship works."

DAY AND NIGHT: Miley and her co-star Emily Osment are close on and off the set—even though they are very different.

BF4L!

Miley's also gotten to be good buds with Ashley Tisdale of *High School Musical*. They both work so much that it's hard for them to see each other. But when they're both around, Miley and Ashley like to have sleepovers with another *High School Musical* actor, Vanessa Hudgens. They order In-and-Out burgers and gorge on Pinkberry frozen yogurt.

DID YOU KNOW?

MILEY'S GOOD-LUCK CHARM IS A RING HER DAD ONCE GAVE TO HER MOM. **It's actually two rings welded together.**

Miley's friends are important to her, and she seems to know what it takes to be a good friend in return. "A true friend is someone who is there for you," Miley said in an interview with *Scholastic Choices*. "I have a song called 'True Friend,' and it says you're supposed to be there through all the ups and downs. There have been a lot of ups, a lot of positive things in my life, but there are things that are not so fun to deal with. A true friend is someone who listens to everything."

The *Best of Both Worlds* tour, and the fame that came along with it, presented Miley with challenges that weren't so fun to deal with. But as the tour came to a close in January of 2008, it had been mostly positive. And the best was yet to come.

THE MOVIE: The *Best of Both Worlds* tour came to an end in January 2008—but fans who missed it could catch the concert film.

iT'S miLEY— in 3-D!

The *Best of Both Worlds* tour hits the big screen— and it's the next best thing to being there.

The *Best of Both Worlds* tour proved one thing to both Disney and the Cyruses: For better or worse, people couldn't get enough of Miley. No matter how big the arenas Miley played, she had to turn away thousands of eager fans.

Disney had a perfect solution to that problem. Why not make a movie of the concert? That way, Miley could perform for millions of people all across the country—at the same time.

MiLeY ON THe BiG SCReeN

Miley agreed to the movie idea, and the production team got to work. For three weeks during the tour, a camera crew caught Miley's every move. They filmed her rocking out onstage. They shot her in rehearsals, goofing around with her dad and her band. They hung around backstage and caught Miley wearing her wig cap and getting her makeup done. They even went into the audience and interviewed fans.

By the time the tour was over, the *Hannah Montana and Miley Cyrus: Best of Both Worlds Concert* movie was done. The premiere on January 17, 2008, was a splashy

Gossip Alert!

Miley's teeth are looking a lot straighter and whiter than they used to! Some suspect Miley has recently gotten porcelain veneers or had her teeth filed and bleached.

Hollywood event, complete with a red carpet and paparazzi flashing their cameras. Miley debuted a new, sophisticated look—"princess-meets-rocker-chic," according to her stylist. She wore dark, smoky eye makeup; a silvery Alberta di Ferretti dress; and wavy, dark hair extensions. "She wanted to get away from the idea of the Hollywood blonde," said Miley's hairstylist, David Medelye, in an interview with *People* magazine.

ON THE RED CARPET

To Miley, the night felt like a dream. "It's the craziest thing to be at your own premiere," she told *US Weekly*. "I'm always walking down other people's carpets! I'm like, 'Hold on a minute! This is my carpet!'"

The Miley movie was a hit from the start. For a cool effect, the film was shown in 3-D, so the audience felt like they were onstage with Miley. "This is better than the front row," Miley told the *Grand Rapids (Mich.) Press*. "You could reach out and feel like you can touch my hand—right there, right in front of you, which is so fun."

To many fans, the movie felt

RED CARPET: Miley shows up for the premiere of *Hannah Montana and Miley Cyrus: Best of Both Worlds Concert* on January 17, 2008.

87

just like being backstage at a Miley concert. People packed the theaters, often dressed like Hannah Montana. They sang along as they peered at the screen through their black-rimmed 3-D glasses. They got to see Miley in rehearsal and crouching beneath the stage as she prepared to make her dramatic entrance. In one scene, Miley almost gets dropped by her dancers during a lift. She's kind of upset and tells Kenny Ortega that she doesn't want to do the lift anymore. Both Kenny and Tish convince Miley that it won't happen anymore, but she has to overcome her fear to do the move again.

For her part, Miley was excited about finally being able to see the show for herself. "I'm a really big perfectionist about what I do, making sure everything is in its place," Miley said to a *Newsweek* reporter. "I was, like, 'Dang, it's finally perfect, and I'm not able to see my own show. I want to see it!' Finally, it was like I was at my own concert, which was wild."

> Miley's really unaffected by all this fame. She is such a sweet girl. She has a hard time [even] telling [waiters] if they get her order wrong.
>
> **TISH CYRUS**
> Miley's mom

OVERHEARD

HOW LONG FOR HannaH?

The movie closed in most theaters by the spring of 2008. But Miley mania had just begun. Wal-Mart announced that they were creating entire mini-Hannah shops inside their mega-stores. There fans could find any Hannah product imaginable—clothes, toys, hair accessories, even cookies and cupcakes. Even better, Disney announced that a new *Hannah Montana* feature film was in the works.

So, how long will Miley's alter ego Hannah stick around? Miley says

T or F

?

Miley's own little sister, Noah Lindsay, once entered a contest to win backstage passes to a *Best of Both Worlds* concert.

No word on whether Noah won the contest!

TRUE!

MOBBED: Miley poses with fans in London.

she wants to do *Hannah* as long as it's popular. But at the same time, there has to be life after the Disney Channel. "*Hannah Montana* is a TV show, so it only goes on for so long," Miley mused in an interview with the *Globe and Mail* of Canada. Could the feature film be Miley's ticket to a career as a movie actor? Or does she have something else up her sleeve?

AMERICA'S IDOL: Miley made a splash at the American Music Awards.

FUTURE SHOCK

Miley does alt-rock? Anything's possible in the post-Hannah world.

Hannah's not going anywhere for a while, but Miley *is* growing up. She knows she won't play Hannah Montana forever. Luckily, she has a lot of options to consider. "I think that you have more opportunities to grow [when you're successful at a young age]," she told *Entertainment Weekly*. "You don't get stuck in one type of film or whatever you are doing. As you grow, all the different things that you can do grow with you."

ROCKiN' ON?

What Miley seems to want most is to expand her music career. She's interested in exploring new styles—more rock, less pop. Miley has said that her influences are all over the charts. She draws inspiration from musicians as different as the Beatles and Kelly Clarkson. Recently, she's been listening to more alternative rock and thinks that might be the direction she'll take in the future.

But Miley the Rocker Chick might be a shock to the Hannah fans of the world, so Miley won't transform herself overnight. "I don't try and put out a bunch of rock music, because obviously that's not my crowd at all," Miley told the *National Post*. "You're not going to start shredding your guitar with a bunch of seven year-olds. But I hope, slowly, I can introduce them to that kind of music."

WHaT NeXT?

So where will Miley go from here? In just a few years, she rocketed from a Tennessee middle-schooler to a certified pop phenomenon. Will she simply fade away

ZOOTOPIA: Miley performs in New Jersey in 2008.

A ROCKER? Miley loves to rock, but she's not ready to shed her pop-star sound.

when she's too old to play Hannah anymore? Will she be able to handle the stress of being a child star? So many other young performers struggle with drug and alcohol problems that ruin their lives and their careers. Miley's challenge is to overcome the odds and find herself a new place as an adult musician with a new set of fans.

"LiFe'S WHaT YOU MaKe iT"

The transition from teen star to serious musician won't be easy, if that's what Miley wants to do. She may have to shed her sweet-as-sugar sound. She'll have to convince record companies and music critics that she can write and sing tunes that an older audience will want to hear. But if anyone can make the switch, Miley can. She's got a down-to-earth attitude and her family at her side. "My mom taught me that the most important thing is staying true to yourself," Miley told *US Weekly*.

So far, Miley seems to have taken her mom's

advice to heart. "Even though I change my hair and I change my makeup and the way I look, I don't change my personality," she told the *National Post*. "And I think [that] shows: You don't need to be someone else to be a rock star, to be cool. You can totally be yourself."

GIVING BACK: Miley poses backstage at the "Idol Gives Back" fundraising special of *American Idol* in L.A. in 2008.

STAR GUiDE

MILEY

Think you know everything about Miley? Keep reading!

STAR STATS

BORN: November 23, 1992

BIRTH NAME: Destiny Hope Cyrus

SIGN: Sagittarius

HOMETOWN: Thompson's Station, TN

SIBLINGS: Noah (sister), Braison (brother), Brandi (half sister), Christopher Cody (half brother), Trace (half brother)

FAVORITE SPORT: Cheerleading

FAVORITE COLORS: Lime green and pink

FAVORITE ALBUM: *Breakaway* by Kelly Clarkson

FAVORITE MOVIE: *Steel Magnolias*

FAVORITE BOOK: *Don't Die, My Love* by Lurlene McDaniel

POP QUIZ

You've read the book— now take the quiz.

1. **Miley was born in . . .**
   a) Georgia
   b) Tennessee
   c) Virginia
   d) Louisiana

2. **When she was little, Miley's family called her . . .**
   a) Smiley
   b) Dusty
   c) Milo
   d) Giggles

3. **The farm that Miley grew up on is called . . .**
   a) Sweet Creek
   b) Singing Hills
   c) Graceland
   d) Rock Springs

4. **When little Miley joined Billy Ray onstage, she liked to sing songs by . . .**
   a) Shania Twain
   b) Elvis Costello
   c) Elvis Presley
   d) Madonna

5. **Miley has dogs named . . .**
   a) Lulu, Bandit, and Penny Lane
   b) Ginger, Bailey, and Beans
   c) Boo, Cocoa, and Caramel
   d) Loco, Juicy, and Minnie Pearl

6. **The idea for the Hannah Montana series was based on an episode from which TV series?**
   a) *That's So Raven*
   b) *Drake and Josh*
   c) *Lizzie McGuire*
   d) *The Naked Brothers Band*

7. **The first name considered for the Hannah Montana character was . . .**
   a) Ashley Dakota
   b) Patty Wyoming
   c) Alexis Texas
   d) Amber December

8. **On the set, Miley likes to snack on . . .**
   a) yogurt with granola, honey, and fresh berries
   b) chocolate-chip cookies
   c) sushi
   d) gummy worms and gummy peach rings

9. **Which person has NOT guest-starred on _Hannah Montana_?**
   a) Corbin Bleu
   b) Amanda Bynes
   c) Joey Fatone
   d) Selena Gomez

10. **The theme of Miley's 15th birthday party was:**
    a) the 1950s
    b) the 1960s
    c) the 1970s
    d) the 1980s

11. **For her 16th birthday, Miley said she wants . . .**
    a) a thoroughbred racehorse
    b) a 1950s Corvette
    c) a trip to Paris with her mom
    d) a motorcycle

12. **The opening night of the _Best of Both Worlds_ tour was in . . .**
    a) St. Louis
    b) Chicago
    c) Nashville
    d) New York City

13. **When on tour, an item on Miley's must-have list is . . .**
    a) an iPod
    b) a travel Bible
    c) a hair straightener
    d) all of the above

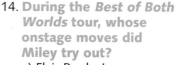

14. **During the _Best of Both Worlds_ tour, whose onstage moves did Miley try out?**
    a) Elvis Presley's
    b) Mick Jagger's
    c) Michael Jackson's
    d) Britney Spears's

15. **Miley is good buds with . . .**
    a) Emily Osment
    b) Mitchel Musso
    c) Ashley Tisdale
    d) all of the above

TIMELINE

MILEY

March 24, 2006
Hannah Montana premieres with Miley in the title role.

September–October 2006 Miley tours with The Cheetah Girls as their opening act.

2005 Miley lands the lead role in Disney's *Hannah Montana* series and moves to L.A.

October 24, 2006
The first *Hannah Montana* soundtrack is released. Miley signs a four-album record deal with Hollywood Records soon after.

2004 Miley becomes the spokesperson for Daisy Rock guitars after she receives a Daisy Rock guitar from her father's fan club.

2003
Tim Burton's movie *Big Fish* premieres with Miley in the part of Ruthie.

November 23, 1992 Miley is born Destiny Hope Cyrus in Nashville, Tennessee.

START HERE

2001 Billy Ray Cyrus lands lead role on PAX cable series, *Doc*. Miley visits her dad while filming in Toronto and becomes interested in acting.

January 30, 2008 Wal-Mart announces that it will carry a line of Hannah Montana clothes, accessories, and food in mini "Hannah Montana shops" in stores.

January 17, 2008 Hannah Montana and Miley Cyrus: Best of Both Worlds Concert movie premieres in Los Angeles. Miley debuts a sophisticated new look.

February 2008 Miley presents the song "That's How You Know" at the Academy Awards.

January 2008 Miley officially changes her name from Destiny Hope Cyrus to Miley Ray Cyrus.

January 2007 The two-millionth copy of the Hannah Montana soundtrack is sold.

December 2007 Miley is ranked number 17 on the *Forbes* magazine Top 20 Earners Under 25 list.

October 18, 2007 The *Best of Both Worlds* concert tour begins in St. Louis, Missouri.

June 26, 2007 The second Hannah Montana soundtrack, Hannah Montana 2: Meet Miley Cyrus, is released.

Summer 2007 Miley dates Nick Jonas of the Jonas Brothers.

awards

MTV Teen Choice Awards, 2007
"Choice TV Actress: Comedy"
"Choice Summer Artist"

Nickelodeon Kids' Choice Awards, 2007
"Favorite TV Actress"

Teen Choice Awards, 2007
"Choice TV Actress—Comedy"

Nickelodeon Kids' Choice Awards, 2008
"Favorite TV Actress"
"Favorite Female Singer"

29th Annual Young Artist Awards, 2008
"Best Performance in a TV Series As a Leading Young Actress"

Gracie Allen Awards, 2008
"Outstanding Female Lead—
    Comedy Series"
    (Children/Adolescent)

DiSCOGRaPHY

STUDIO ALBUMS
Hannah Montana (soundtrack), 2006, multi-platinum
Hannah Montana 2: Meet Miley Cyrus (double-disc
  soundtrack), 2007, multi-platinum
Hannah Montana 2: Non-Stop Dance Party, 2008
Breakout, 2008

SINGLES (AS MILEY)
"**G.N.O. (Girls' Night Out)**," *Hannah Montana 2:
  Meet Miley Cyrus*, disc 2, 2007
"**I Miss You**," *Hannah Montana 2: Meet Miley Cyrus*, disc 2, 2007
"**See You Again**," *Hannah Montana 2:
  Meet Miley Cyrus*, disc 2, 2007
"**Start All Over**," *Hannah Montana 2:
  Meet Miley Cyrus*, disc 2, 2007
"**Ready, Set, Don't Go**," *Home at Last*
  (with Billy Ray Cyrus), 2007
"**Let's Dance**," *Hannah Montana 2: Meet Miley Cyrus*, disc 2, 2008
"**All Eyes on Me**," 2008
"**7 Things**," *Breakout*, 2008

SINGLES (AS HANNAH)
"**I Got Nerve**," *Hannah Montana*, 2006
"**If We Were a Movie**," *Hannah Montana*, 2006
"**Just Like You**," *Hannah Montana*, 2006
"**The Best of Both Worlds**," *Hannah Montana*, 2006
"**The Other Side of Me**," *Hannah Montana*, 2006
"**This Is the Life**," *Hannah Montana*, 2006
"**Pumpin' Up the Party**," *Hannah Montana*, 2006
"**Who Said**," *Hannah Montana*, 2006
"**Rockin' Around the Christmas Tree**,"
  Hannah Montana (Holiday Edition), 2006

"**Bigger Than Us**," *Hannah Montana 2:*
  Meet Miley Cyrus, disc 1, 2007
"**Life's What You Make It**," *Hannah Montana 2:*
  Meet Miley Cyrus, disc 1, 2007
"**Make Some Noise**," *Hannah Montana 2:*
  Meet Miley Cyrus, disc 1, 2007
"**Nobody's Perfect**," *Hannah Montana 2:*
  Meet Miley Cyrus, disc 1, 2007
"**One in a Million**," *Hannah Montana 2:*
  Meet Miley Cyrus, disc 1, 2007
"**True Friend**," *Hannah Montana 2: Meet Miley Cyrus,* disc 1, 2007
"**We Got the Party**," *Hannah Montana 2:*
  Meet Miley Cyrus, disc 1, 2007
"**Rock Star**," 2008

SOUNDTRACKS
"**Zip-A-Dee-Doo-Dah**," *DisneyMania 4,* 2006
"**Part of Your World**," *DisneyMania 5,* 2006
"**I Learned From You**," *Bridge to Terabithia,* 2007
"**We Got the Party**," *Jonas Brothers: Bonus Jonas Edition/*
  Hannah Montana 2: Rock Star Edition, 2007

MUSIC VIDEOS
"**Start All Over**," 2007

TOURS
The Party's Just Begun Tour, opening act for
  The Cheetah Girls, 2007
Best of Both Worlds Tour, 2007–2008

Fan Sites

HANNAH MONTANA OFFICIAL SITE
http://tv.disney.go.com/disneychannel/hannahmontana

The Disney Channel's *Hannah Montana* web-site introduces the show's stars, provides an episode guide, free mini-video games, and more.

MILEY CYRUS OFFICIAL SITE
www.mileycyrus.com

At Miley's authorized official website, fans can read the most current Miley news, view a photo gallery, find Miley's schedule, and take a virtual tour of Miley's concert bus.

More to Read

Alexander, Lauren. **Mad for Miley: An Unauthorized Biography.** New York: Price Stern Sloan, 2007. (128 pages)

Janic, Susan. **Living the Dream: Hannah Montana and Miley Cyrus.** Toronto: ECW Press, 2008. (144 pages)

Kent, Brittany. **Miley Cyrus: This Is Her Life.** New York: Berkley Trade, 2008. (192 pages)

Leavitt, Amy Jane. **Miley Cyrus (Robbie Readers).** Hockessin, Del.: Mitchell Lane Publishers, 2007. (32 pages)

Robb, Jackie. **Miley Mania! Behind the Scenes With Miley Cyrus (Star Scene).** New York: Scholastic Inc., 2008. (48 pages)

alter ego *noun* a second self

alternative *adjective* different from what is usual

anticipation *noun* the act of looking forward to something

aspiring *adjective* in the process of seeking to accomplish a particular goal

choreography *noun* the art of creating and arranging dance steps and movements

clamor *noun* a strongly expressed demand, often loudly and by many people all at once

controversy *noun* prolonged and heated disagreement

diabetes *noun* a disease in which the body has trouble controlling the amount of sugar in the blood

ebullience *noun* the quality of being cheerful and having lots of energy

ecstatic *adjective* extremely happy

frenetic *adjective* fast and energetic in a wild and uncontrolled way

inspiration *noun* someone or something that influences a person creatively

intrigued *adjective* fascinated or very interested

mortifying *adjective* incredibly embarrassing

paparazzi *noun* photographers who pursue celebrities to get photographs of them

phenomenon *noun* something very unusual and remarkable

potential *adjective* possible but not yet actual

precocious *adjective* very advanced in intelligence or maturity for one's age

premiere *noun* the first public performance of a movie or play

scrutiny *noun* very careful observation or examination

stability *noun* the state of being steady, safe, and secure

veteran *adjective* experienced in a particular field of work

MILEY
INDEX

ABOUT THE AUTHOR

Emma Carlson Berne has written over a dozen fiction and nonfiction books for children and young adults, including several biographies. Her other biographical subjects have included the Hilton sisters, the rapper Snoop Dogg, Christopher Columbus, Frida Kahlo, Sacagawea, and Helen Keller. Emma lives in Cincinnati, Ohio, where she is at work on a young-adult romance novel.